The Road to Empatheia

Introductory

Every human being, should they live long enough, will eventually reach a certain point in their lives, a time of spiritual growth in which the recognition that the things that happen, your circumstances, by choice or chance were necessary for soul evolution, but not entirely in your control. Other forces perhaps, beyond the veil of our limited perceptions and understanding, forces ethereal or outside of the terrestrial world, but it seems every living thing leaves a small fracture upon the path we lay forth in our short time here.

It's a road we all share, though many never see it through. It's our choice to be an obstacle or to light the way for others.

It's a road to love and acceptance,
To Empatheia.

Empatheia is not a place, but a state of mind, a way and should you embark upon it you'll see there everyone is smiling

…and free.

-

The fragments of thought in the pages that follow came about through much life experience and my unbiased interest in philosophy and the spiritual compiled over the last ninety days as they came to me. Some themes and ideas are repeated as nothing was excluded, but the small talk.

God gave you a mind.

Ponder these things.

-

✧

I once thought my anger
Was a sign of toughness,
But time and circumstance
Have led me to the
Realization that it is a
Weakness that brought
Much ruin to my life.

✧

We can be taught knowledge,
But wisdom is (l)earned.

✧

Trial by fire, the
Trials of the flesh

✧

I've learned many things
From the human animal
As well as the wild ones,
But my greatest teacher
Thus far has been the
Trees,
Unmoved by the opinions
Of others and needing
Only what nature provides.

✧

All is forgotten over time,
Succumb to oblivion and
Will be remembered only
By those that bury it.

Therefore heedlessly
Chasing fame and
Immense wealth are the
Goals of a low-minded
Fool.

We all must learn the
Hard way. Talk is
Ignored in youth,
Sins are tested, we
Kiss venomous
Snakes and
Jump into fire.

Those that marry too
Young are often willing
To risk everything
They've built with their
Spouse for the
Momentary impulses

Of a teenager.

In women this usually
Occurs in their mid-
Thirties to early forties.
The husband strays or
Stops paying attention,
Etc…

As for men, well,
Most of them cheat.

One should awaken
Early, before dawn,
As not to miss that
Quiet time of nature's
Inherent beauty,
Whispering winds, a
Variety of bird chatter,
Even the scent of the
Cool air, before the
Bustle and stink of
Mankind distorts it all.

✧

When we reach the elder stage
Our minds become childlike,
Closer to spirit, we've learned

...to let go

✧

Man wasn't meant to be
In the air or the water, we're
Earthborn creatures and
To the Earth we shall return.

✧

It dawned upon me
That my path to
Self-destruction was
Not so much
Sociopathy, but an
Inborn resistance

To conformity.

✧

The size of their bank
Account, their home or
Their occupational/
Social status,

The unfulfilling goals
Of the fool.

Like dogs chasing their
Tails.

✧

Thoughts manifest.
Things disappear.

Your soul …to the sky,
Your body …to the Earth.

✧

What's birthed from the vagina
Appears no different than that
From out of the anus.

✧

I don't necessarily
Fault them, they're but
Locked into a program
As I once was.

[a slave to my impulses and
Possessed by my possessions]

✧

If one is a whore,
So shall their sons or
Daughters be and

If one is a brute, so

They shall be, if not
The victim of one.

The law of Karma.

Though birth and death
Are a part of nature, thus
God's work and
Beyond my control.

I accept these things.

◇

If you think you're above
...or entitled,
...or should you know
Someone who does,
Remember, any of us,
No matter how virtuous
Can cease to exist at
Any moment, therefore
No one is special, but a
Small piece of a
Collective
Of third density beings
Condemned to suffer

On a small planet
Within a vast universe,
Thus

Insignificant.

✧

My reluctance to go
With the flow of life,
With nature, shattered
My heart and mind.

Now I've gathered the
Better parts of
Myself and arose much
Stronger like a phoenix

…just in time for the end.

✧

By God's will and my own
I have chosen, therefore

I am free.

It's like a veil was
Lifted and I no longer
See the good in others,
Only what they show me
Which is generally
Commonplace and
Often self-serving.

Fear not the transition,
But to die within the
Concrete tomb of a
Corporation.
Crawl beneath a tree
If you must.

Too much "drink"
Gives me desires
I don't need to
Understand.

✧

Dwelling in the past,
Trying to relive the "good times"
Is like searching a landfill
For a receipt you've discarded.

✧

Live now, not in dead yesterdays,
Nor fantastical futures, which
Were never promised in the first place.

✧

We're all students in the

School of life until we die,
Learning, growing.
Those that think they know
Everything because they've
Attained society's standard
Of getting married young,
Accumulating possessions,
Having children and in
About ten years growing
Tired of it all, turning to
Inebriation or adultery
Like every other lost soul
Since the dawn of time
Are like the lumps of clay
Soon to cover them.

God didn't give me this
Brain to waste away
Chasing fruitless desires,
Mindless pleasures or
Trying to force love from
Women that don't love
Their spouse, their
Children or even
Themselves, foolishly

Thinking they could love
Me and not repeat their
Performance.

✧

I had to learn the hard way,
But that's still preferable to
Having never learned at all.

Many never do.

✧

People are all the same,
Men and women alike.
Very few break from the
Herd and if you're not like
Them, they'll attempt to
Bring you down.

Their lives are dull.
You have an edge.
They're not sharp enough to lead.

Thus, why they follow.

◇

If you've expectations
Of anyone outside of
Yourself,

You've already failed.

◇

Make no mistake,
I feel nothing toward them.
I needed their jealousy and
Aversion in order to grow.
My soul evolved, rebelled.
Where I could've fought
The charges against me,

I chose freedom to slavery.

◇

One must choose and not be chosen.

◇

No more robotic movements, everything flowing.

No past, no future, only moments in time.

◇

It appears to me now that
The only external paradise
To be found is within those
Sacred forested places
Where man is forbidden
To build.

There are no good or
Bad people,
We all have a shadow.

Some integrate it,
Others are consumed.

Anyone that has
Heightened your senses
As they've crossed
Your timeline was your
Teacher.

✧

Those we see
…and hear
…and smell
…and taste
…and feel,
The most significant in our growth.

In time we discard the
Five senses and
Return to spirit.

✧

Everything happens
For a reason.
We are to learn from
All we encounter,

Those that hurt
As well as
Those that heal.

◇

Take it all in,
  The Sun,
    The Trees,
      The birds,
Things of true beauty,
          Of no regret.

◇

Ever-learning and
Moving ideas
In and out.

◇

I accept how people are,
Even my own flaws, but
They too must accept that

The Eagle flies alone.

✧

Everything is connected,
Stuck here on Earth.

Better to help and
Not hinder.

✧

The first steps to freedom
Are in choosing.

I made a conscious effort
To take back my mind
Pathetically controlled
By others.

To forgive, but never forget.

◇

I don't look at things
In terms of
Accomplishments and
Failures anymore.

◇

Like a serpent I've shed
All of those old skins, old
Titles, I long to be a free
Man and nothing more.

◇

When you appear lowly
In the eyes of the sheep and
You're indifferent to the fact,

You're on your way to freedom.

✧

How quickly people turn.

✧

The moment you've
Nothing to offer them
Monetarily or you're
No longer balancing
On the top rung of the
Social ladder they
Ostracize you.
It all doesn't seem
Much different from
High school.
It all repeats in the
Cycles of life,
Fads and failure,
Popularity and exile.

✧

Praised today, blamed
Tomorrow.
Everyone's lot

…lest they reach the
Next stage, step beyond
The matrix and
Stop the chase.

✧

There's nothing to be found.

✧

The Trees have taught me
The power of silence, calmness
In the face of adversity and

…to give.

◇

Birth = Fluid | Death = Ash/Smoke
(Vapor)

◇

If only I'd thought with
Reason back in school
The pitiful bullies wouldn't
Have gotten the best of me,
Made me feel less than them.

If only I'd thought,

These idiots that cling to
Their popularity will
Wrinkle and die like
Everyone else and their
Followers will eventually
Follow them into the
Grave and they too
Shall be forgotten.

All is forgotten and
Consigned to oblivion.

✧

Many will never see the
Hopeless cycle of pain
That is chasing pleasure.

✧

Until we can relinquish
Fear as well as hope and
Accept everything as it is,

Hamsters on a wheel.

✧

To be a good man and
Not to boast about it.

✧

L_iving
O_utside
V_iolent
E_ngagements

✧

Having a faith or a
Religion can be an
Uplifting and positive
Experience, but one
Must be careful with
Congregations.
History has shown that
It takes but one fanatic to
Rally easily manipulated
People into cult-like
Tendencies.

✧

To respect others and
Live your teachings
As long as they don't
Harm another living thing.

Our relationship to God
Is to each their own and
You lead by example,
Not by useless chatter.

When you think of all the
Great people in your family
Or another's
Or the children and
Animals that touched your
Heart, How transitory our
Relations to them are,
How swiftly they can
Disappear, how attached
We can be and the
Tremendous pain it causes.
It makes you appreciate what
Little time we have with
Them, but to remember that

Everything mortal comes and
Goes.
Keep good in your heart and
Mind.

✧

No coincidence. Not all changes are.

✧

Cowards need scapegoats, men accept
responsibility.

✧

Nothing new. Look at history,
Men and women have always
Acted in such ways.

✧

Be content with the hand
You've been dealt, the lot
You've been cast.

✧

That I've reached another
Stage in my evolution is
Very well, but no one is
Better than anyone else,
Just at different stages of
Development.

✧

The light of the Sun,
Unpolluted air,
The scent of trees:

Things I value most.

✧

The original people had a
Close connection to the
"Sky Elders" or as we've
Labeled them
Extraterrestrials.

✧

Marriage,
Boredom,
Betrayal,
Divorce,
Repeat.

The same now as before.

So why stress?

Read.
Know the real history
Of the wicked world.
It's all been done before,

All common,
All stupid.

I've had many pleasures in this life,
Many lessons.

Unrefined men will insert
Their penis into anyone and

Most modern women
Eventually get bored and
Cheat.

Why all the fuss?
They follow, even in the
Absence of a shepherd.

Technology-
Some useful, but most,
Garbage, a trap, made
People lazier, more
Selfish and easier to be
Fraudulent or to
Manipulate.

Few understood my
Poetry and I anticipate
Few will understand my
Philosophy of life.

Matters little.

Everyone is forgotten,
Those that love you and
Those that hate you as well.

Shadows and dust.

[Mind/Body - Balanced]
[Spirit -   Elevated]

✧

The Teachings of the Trees:

- Born of Earth, still reach for the Heavens
- Carbon dioxide to Oxygen (purpose)
- Competing for sunlight, yet sharing soil
- Unmoved from their nature, their destiny
- Unlike people, they listen more than they speak

✧

Focus on the journey,
Not the outcome.

Be present.

✧

We build better monuments
To house the dead than
We do the living.

✧

I've been the cause of
All my suffering, through
Thought, word and deed.

✧

Whatever God and nature
Have woven into the fabric
Of my existence, the threads
Of my timeline, I accept.

✧

I can never go back,
Nor would I want to.

✧

I choose freedom
Even if that means death.

✧

Embrace the Reaper,
The transition to nowhere.

Life is short and
Beyond your control
Lest you suicide.

Take no pride in any
Living thing's suffering
Be it plant, animal or man.

I once asked a scientist
Why we don't test drugs on
Rapists and murderers?

Surely the worst human
Beings don't deserve
Better treatment than

Animals that are merely
Following their natural
Order.

To observe and reflect.
(Reflection only to learn,
One mustn't linger too
Long or you'll face
Depression.

Stay present.
Always.

A woman's essence can
Be just as intoxicating as
The drink and can make
Men say and do the same
Stupid things.

✧

We can be taught like
Chimpanzees, but
No one really learns
Anything until they've
Been knifed in the back
Or licked by the flames
Of deceit.

✧

Through copious amounts of pain we grow and

With even the smallest amount of love we find
strength

…to carry on.

✧

Our lives are always in flux,
In transition, constant change

…like seasons in New York,
…like planetary orbits,
…Empires,
…Emotions,
…Everything.

✧

From nowhere to life
To death to nowhere

Or perhaps reincarnation
To finish the lessons for
That particular soul through
A new incarnation.

Something to ponder.

✧

To never stray from the path.

✧

Expect the unexpected.
Nothing is what it seems,
No one
Who they say.

✧

Other forces at work, spirits or
Benign beings from other worlds,
Dimensions.

✧

Have no expectations nor
Assumptions of others.
You'll most certainly be
Let down.

✧

The human experience is
Quite strange and comes
With much suffering, but
What does one expect?
It's merely a rotting vessel
For to carry the soul while
It learns on its return trip
To nowhere or rebirth.
(Does any mortal man
Really know?)

Another human's praise
Or blame has no merit.
Look at what drives them and
Forgive their ignorance.

Exiled.

I've a heart, a mind and
Free will.

Herein lies the problem.

✧

Sometimes to lose is to win.

✧

Once you reach a certain
Age, you begin to see how
Everything repeats,
Art, fashion, everything.

Many never notice blindly
Following everyone else and
Every lame trend.

Either the Matrix exists
Through our collective
Thoughts or we through it.

✧

Politicians care less for
Your well being than your
Worst enemies.
Stay away from politics.
Delve rather, into poetry,
Philosophy or spirituality,
Things that spark the soul.

Display kindness, but don't
Be taken advantage of.

✧

I suppose that's the plight
Of all free-thinking men and
Women, never to be
Understood till long after
Our moment of mortality.

✧

Don't put too much
Emphasis on what others
Say. They'll praise you
One day and blame you
Another having no
Direction themselves.

✧

The poor have always
Outnumbered the wealthy,
Yet they've rarely mustered
A rebellion.
Too easily divided.

✧

The sheep will follow,
The eagle flies away.

✧

Think to yourself,
These miserable morons
Are judging me?
Then laugh, for the followers
Are really dead before
They've died and
Surely forgotten.

✧

Plant seeds of truth and see what grows.

✧

Vengeance is truth,
…is distance,
…is best served slightly
Chilled with a slice of
Intelligence.

✧

To walk among the
Deceased where the
Stones pray to a living
God.

✧

The suffering, the light or
Truth at the end of the
Tunnel, comes only by
Delving into the darkness,
Tasting the flames that
Consume you over time,
This Hellish life running
In circles, chasing desires,
Vying for comfort and
Endless pleasure.

To come out of the
Darkness

…Stronger.

✧

Karma:

Look at the way the world
Was shaped over time
Through slavery and war.

You could die tragically
This very moment, do you
Want your last thoughts
To be on such useless and
Trivial things or that
Which you love and
Loves you in return.

Attempt to make someone
Smile today and speak no
Lies and see what happens.

✧

Social constructs repress our true nature.

✧

Practice what you preach.
Stray from preaching what
You practice,

Lead the way.

✧

Dwelling too often in the
Past was my weakness,
Though time for reflection
Gave me strength.

✧

Don't squander your time
Trying to discourse with
Unlearned or unrefined
Imbeciles.

Better to be silent than
Wasting words.

If the blind majority follow
Some new ideal
It's probably not anything
Good.

Man's inability to accept
Everything that happens
In the course of his short
Existence only adds
Unnecessary suffering
To an already painful life.

The more one accepts his
Lot, the less resistance.

✧

Death:

When all of the
Pleasures and pains
Of this prison of flesh
Subside.

✧

It's just like leaving an
Equestrian event, all
Thorobreds,
Harness nags and
Horseshit.

✧

Upon awakening one
Begins to see how they
Strategically place liquor
Stores and whores on nearly
Every street corner in
Nearly every city.

As our minds expand our elder's regress.

We learn many vital lessons
In the brevity of our lives and
Still we die never really grasping
Anything.

Overly ambitious or

Completely lacking, like
Those of political beliefs
Leaning toward one side
Or the other, giving up
One ideal only to be
Enslaved by another.

Still following, never free.

Another occupation
   Comes to an end,

…another relationship,

…another life.

All the same,
All forgotten,
All covered with the
Dirt of time and

If you lucky enough
They'll kick some dirt
Over your corpse.

If not, well, you'll feed
Coyotes, vultures and
Worms.

No worse than the years
You've spent feeding
Ungrateful humans.

✧

I laugh at the pretentious,
All-knowing because they
Attended college and
Watch television.

Even monkeys can study,
Mimic and
Watch television.

Try formulating your own
Thoughts.

Easier to eat, shit and
Procreate like monkeys.

✧

When a fighter is behind
In competition and he
Gains the strength to come
Back and win they say he
Had to "dig deep".
I think that's the same for
Many aspects of life.

Relationships for example,
When we're too attached
To another person and
They depart or ascend,
We have to dig deep to
Find the strength to carry on.

On the other hand, when
One is betrayed or
Heartbroken from loss of
Love, one can dig deep or
Retreat into the trenches
Of the mind and see
Beyond the blinders,
Everything for what it is,
What they really are:

Bumbling idiots and

Unfaithful drunken pigs.

What do the opinions of
Idiots and pigs amount to?

Nothing.

Artificial Intelligence:

An appropriate moniker,
For only a moron needs a
Robot to think for them.

Technological advancements
Can be good as history has
Shown, but much of it has
Afforded us too much
Comfort and convenience
Which subsequently led to
The gluttony and sloth

Of the modern world.

$\diamond$

History never changes, only the names.

$\diamond$

A world of imbalance,
Kept that way
By those in control.

$\diamond$

Everything Ends.

"No labour is good but that Which aims at producing Courage and strength of soul Rather than of body."

- Diogenes